Here's what people have to say about the
Jannah Jewels Adventure Book Series:

I can't continue without saying it one more time: Powerful Young Muslim Girls! No damsels in distress, no dominating male protagonist, no cliché girly nonsense! ... This is exactly what our girls need to grow up reading.
–Emma Apple, author of best-selling 'Children's First Questions' Series

Learning about Islamic history and famous Muslims of the past makes these books a historical book lover's wish, and the Islamic twist is a plus for young Muslim readers. Jannah Jewels has been Muslimommy approved as kid-friendly!
-Zakiyya Osman, MusliMommy.com

I love all of the Jannah Jewels books, and the fact that you combine history and adventure in your stories. I also liked that you put the holy verses of Quran that remind us to stay close to Allah and I liked the fact that in one book you mentioned the verse from Quran which mentions the benefit of being kind to your enemy. I have read all of the Jannah Jewels books and even read two of these books in one day, that's how much I like these books!
–Fatima Bint Saifurrehman, 8 Years Old

I could really feel the love that went into this book – the characters, the places, the history, and the things that the author clearly strongly believes in and wants to share with our children and the wider world through her heroines…My daughter's verdict? "I would give the book a 10 out of 10 mum"
–Umm Salihah, HappyMuslimah.com Blog

Fantastic book! My child was turning pages and couldn't wait to read the next chapter. So much so he's asking for the next book in the series.
-Mrs. S. A. Khanom, Book Reviewer

This was a great book with a nice story. I am happy to say that all three of my daughters (ages 13, 8 & 6) fell in love with it and can't wait for the next installment. My daughters could relate to the characters and have read the book several times.
–Jessica Colon, Book Reviewer

It's wonderful to see young Muslim women defined for who they are, their strengths and talents, and not for what's on their head.
–Kirstin, Woodturtle Blog

My kids liked the characters because they are modest in their mannerisms and dress, so that was something my daughter could relate to. Even though the characters are girls, it had enough excitement and the presence of supporting male characters to be read by both girls and boys. Throughout the book there was an essence of Islamic values and there was a lot of adventure to keep us guessing!
-HomeStudyMama, Book Reviewer

So inspirational... The young girls in these series are defined by the strength of their character. These non-stereotyped female role models are what our girls (& boys) need to read about. The storyline is engaging and subtly teaches moral lessons. Highly recommend these books.
-Amn, Book Reviewer

It's important for girls and boys, Muslim and not, to have strong, non-stereotyped female role models. Jannah jewels bring that in a unique way with a twist on time travel, fantasy, super heroes and factual Muslim history. It is beautifully written, engaging and an absolute must for any Muslim (and non-Muslim) kids library! My daughter LOVES The Jannah Jewels...
–Hani, Book Reviewer

We've reviewed 100s of Islamic non-fiction and fiction books from every single continent, except Antarctica, and none of the fiction books have made such an impression on our family as Jannah Jewels.
–Ponn M. Sabra, Best-selling author, AmericanMuslimMom.com

By Tayyaba Syed & Umm Nura

Vancouver

This book is for my mother whose prayers have carried me here and beneath whose feet I continuously find jewels of Jannah.
–T.S.

Thank you to my Amejaan whose prayers are the sweet breeze in my sail as I journey through this ocean of life to the next. – U.N.

Published by Gentle Breeze Books, Vancouver, B.C., Canada

Copyright 2015 by Umm Nura
Illustrations by Nayzak Al-Hilali

Visit us on the Web! www.JannahJewels.com

ISBN:978-0-9867208-9-5

September 2015

Contents

Sport:

Archery

Role:

Guides and leads the girls

Superpower:

Intense sight and spiritual insight

Fear:

Spiders

Special Gadget:

Ancient Compass

Carries:

Bow and Arrow, Ancient Map, Compass

HIDAYAH

JAIDE

Sport:

Skateboarding

Role:

Artist, Racer

Superpower:

Fast racer on foot or skateboard

Fear:

Hunger (She's always hungry!)

Special Gadget:

Time Travel Watch

Carries:

Skateboard, Sketchpad, Pencil, Watch

Sport:

Horseback Riding

Role:

Walking Encyclopedia, Horseback Rider

Superpower:

Communicates with animals

Fear:

Heights

Special Gadget:

Book of Knowledge

Carries:

Book of Knowledge, has horse named "Spirit"

Sport:

Swimming

Role:

Environmentalist, Swimmer

Superpower:

Breathes underwater for a long time

Fear:

Drowning

Special Gadget:

Metal Ball

Carries:

Sunscreen, Water canteen, Metal Ball

SUPPORTING CHARACTERS

JAFFAR

JASMIN

FATIMA AL-FIHRI

THE JANNAH JEWELS ADVENTURE 6

MOROCCO

ARTIFACT 6: A DARK-COLORED OVAL OBJECT

"When you face darkness, know that Allah is An-Nur and will bring you into light."
~ Master Swimmer

As salaamu alaikum Dear Readers,

We feel truly blessed to be embarking on this great journey with you all in the Jannah Jewels' newest adventure! Hidayah, Iman, Jaide and Sara have become a part of our homes and feel just like family!

Seeing the world from all corners is a dream that we share. We were both blessed to visit Morocco and the ancient city of Fes, as well as surrounding cities of Marrakech, Casablanca, Tangier & Meknes.

The city of Fes in Morocco holds deep history and beautiful serenity. You will learn about Fatima al-Fihri, the founder of the first university in the world, al-Qarawiyine, in this book. We are sure you will appreciate Fatima al-Fihri's amazing efforts after reading Book 6!

Thank you for being a part of it all, dear Reader. With your dedication, we have reached halfway in the Jannah Jewels Adventure Series!

May Peace be with you,
Umm Nura & Tayyaba Syed

Prologue

Long ago, there was a famous archer who mastered the way of the Bow and Arrow. He was given the enormous task of protecting the world from evil. He was a peaceful archer, who knew an important secret that made him extremely powerful; not only in archery but also in other ways you would not believe. The secret was written inside a scroll, placed in a box, and locked away inside a giant Golden Clock to be protected from the hands of evil.

But the Master Archer was growing old, and the time had come to pass on his duty to an apprentice. He watched his students carefully every day. The students trained extra hard to earn the Master Archer's approval. Two students caught the Master Archer's eye: Khan and Layla. Khan was fierce in his fights, made swift strategies and had strong hands. Layla was flawless in her aim, light on her feet and had intense vision. Khan wanted to be the next Master Archer more than anything in the world. Layla, on the other hand, just wanted peace in the world, no matter who became the next Master Archer. Finally, the day dawned when a new Master had to emerge. Despite everyone's surprise and for the first time in history, the duty was given to a girl—Layla. Layla trained relentlessly and over time proved her just and peaceful nature. The Master Archer said, "It is only the humble, the peaceful and those who can control their anger that are allowed to possess the secrets of the bow and arrow."

Before long, Khan and Layla were married and practiced the way of the Bow and Arrow together. In time, they had two children, a boy named Jaffar and a girl named Jasmin.

Jaffar grew up to be a curious and gentle spirit who loved to practice calligraphy, read books, and sit for long hours under shaded trees. Jasmin, on the other hand, liked to play sports, tumble in the grass, and copy her mother in archery. They all lived peacefully together in the old, walled city of Fez in Morocco, *or so it seemed*.

Khan fought with Jaffar, his son, every day, urging him to work harder at archery. Had it been up to Jaffar, he would simply have sat for hours reading his books and practicing calligraphy. He was just not interested in archery, but his father was so fierce that Jaffar had no choice but to practice with his sister, Jasmin, who was a natural. As the days went on, trouble brewed, and gloom and misery settled upon the villa's walls. Over time, Jaffar grew to be an outstanding archer, fierce and powerful, much like his father, despite his not wanting to do so, and soon forgot all about his reading and writing. On the other hand, Layla practiced archery differently. She practiced to refine her skills and herself; she never used archery for fighting, but for strength-building and purifying her heart. Soon, this difference in practicing the Bow and Arrow caused problems for everyone.

*   *   *   *

Far away in Vancouver, Canada, Hidayah was sitting in her classroom, bored as usual. She had always thought that nothing exciting ever happened, but this day everything was about to change. Hidayah was walking home from school when she spotted a mysterious woman in the neighbourhood park.

3

The woman was wearing dark red, flowing robes, and something behind her sparkled in the sunlight. It looked as though she were moving into the empty house on the hill. No one had ever lived there for as long as Hidayah could remember.

Hidayah decided she was done with being bored. So she started the long trek up to the house on the hill. She huffed up the porch stairs and tiptoeing, looked in one of the windows. She couldn't believe what she saw! It was the woman in long, dark red, flowing robes with a bow and arrow in her hands, standing so completely still that she looked like a wax statue. Her strong hands were wrapped around the bow, and her eyes were intently gazing at the target across the room. She was so focused and still that Hidayah had to hold her breath afraid of making any sound. Hidayah sat mesmerized waiting for the woman to let go of the arrow. *But she did not let go.*

So it happened that day after day, Hidayah would hurry up the hill to watch this mysterious woman. And every day she came closer and closer to the door of the house. Several months went by in this way until one day; Hidayah finally mustered enough courage to sit on the doorstep. Then, for the first time, the woman let go of the arrow, which landed in a perfect spot right in the center of the target. The woman turned and said, "So, you have come." She looked right into Hidayah's eyes as though she was looking through her. Hidayah, at first startled, regained her calmness and with her head lowered said, "My name is Hidayah, may I be your student? Can you teach me the Bow and Arrow?" And the woman replied, "I accepted you as my student the very first day you peeked through the window." Thus, Hidayah trained with the Master Archer for several years and was on her way to becoming a very strong, yet gentle, archer.

1

Answers

Hidayah could not help but toss and turn in bed. She had hardly slept. Her mind was racing from the intensity of their last mission. Being stuck in ancient Spain and then moving forward in time 200 years was not at all what the Jannah Jewels had expected to happen. It was their most difficult mission yet. After much trial and error, the Jannah Jewels had correctly identified which two substances were needed as artifacts to be placed in the Golden Clock at 4 and 5 o'clock.

The Jannah Jewels had feared they might not return home to Vancouver from ancient Spain. What if they never saw their families and loved ones again or ate their favorite foods?

Hidayah did not mind the idea of being lost in time, though, as much as her friends Iman, Jaide, and Sara did. They were not orphans like her. They had families and homes to call their own.

Nevertheless, Hidayah could not help but worry about what their next mission would be like, at least for her friends' sake. She knew her archery teacher, Sensei Elle, would be sending them somewhere back into time and space again soon.

The Master Archer, Sensei Elle had accepted Hidayah as her student several years ago at the top of the hill in her dojo. But, still, no one knew from where Sensei had come or if she even had any family of her own. To Hidayah, Sensei did feel like family, and she was the main reason Hidayah wanted to return back from all previous missions thus far. She was grateful Sensei chose her and her friends out of all the other dojo students to be the Jannah Jewels and find the 12 artifacts. As risky and dangerous as the missions had been, Hidayah, Iman, Jaide, and Sara came back stronger physically and spiritually each time meeting amazing scholars along the way.

As Hidayah laid on her right side, tired from a long day of training, she wondered where their next destination would be and which era of history they would have to encounter. She gazed at her bow and arrow resting against the purple painted walls of her bedroom. She thought about having to face Jaffar, Jasmin, Moe and Slim again on the next mission. Whatever it took, she was not going to let them open the Golden Clock first and discover the hidden secret that was locked inside. At last, Hidayah had fallen into a deep and peaceful sleep.

Whomp! Whomp! WHOMP!

Whomp! Whomp! WHOMP!

Hidayah shot up in bed, as her heart began to race. She scratched her head. "I have got to find a nicer way to wake up than this sound!" Hidayah said to herself. She reached and turned her clock to face her: 3:00 a.m. It was *Tahajjud* time.

"And of the night, prostrate yourself to Him and glorify Him during the long night."

Hidayah remembered her Sensei reciting this verse from the *Holy Qur'an* and teaching her the power of the *Tahajjud* prayer.

"There is a time in the last third of the night that God descends to the lowest Heaven and asks His Angels which of His servants is asking of Him," Sensei Elle had told Hidayah. "This is an invitation from your Lord and an opportunity for accepted *du'a*. It is the fuel that will help you overcome any obstacle you face."

Hidayah brushed her teeth, made *wudhu*, threw on her prayer clothes over her pajamas, and stepped with her right foot onto her prayer rug. She took a deep breath, cleared her heart and mind, and began to pray. Immediately, her shoulders relaxed, her breath steadied and her worries melted away.

Only God can help us get through this, and I know He will, she thought to herself with renewed confidence.

After sitting and making quiet supplications to her Lord for help and guidance on their next adventure, the silence of the night was interrupted by the birds' melodious chirping outside her window.

"The morning has come," she whispered to

9

herself with a smile.

She quickly slipped on her red sweatshirt, joggers and red *hijab*. She grabbed her bow and arrow and quietly climbed down the stairs out of the house. Hidayah laced up her sneakers and swiftly ran up to Sensei Elle's home at the top of the hill. She loved how the air felt different this early in the morning. She breathed in the extra coolness and freshness. As she reached the dojo, other students were trickling in as well under the pink sky. The Sensei's home had become their dojo for training as well as a sanctuary for worship.

Hidayah slipped off her shoes and scanned the group of girls as they lined up for the morning *Fajr* prayer. The other Jannah Jewels were not in sight.

That is not like them, Hidayah thought.

Just then Iman, Jaide, and Sara entered the prayer area from the kitchen. They were bringing in trays of mint tea and snacks. They spotted Hidayah, and each of them gave her a welcoming smile.

"Hey that's my job!" Hidayah complained as she walked up to her best friends. She was known in the dojo for making the best mint green tea with honey.

"The early bird catches the blessings!" Sara teased while kneeling and carefully placing a tray of tiny glasses onto the low table.

"Don't worry. I tasted it, and nothing beats your tea," Jaide reassured Hidayah.

"Hey!" Iman protested.

The four girls giggled and joined the front row for prayer. A sense of relief came over Hidayah after seeing her friends so calm despite the difficult mission they had recently faced in Andalusia. She felt her prayers already being answered.

Bismillah! Bring on the next mission, she thought. *With Allah by our side, we can do anything!*

2

Close to Home

"I can't do this anymore, Uncle," Jaffar complained to his Uncle Idris. "I don't know how, but these Jannah Jewels keep beating me!"

"If you can't beat 'em, join 'em," advised his uncle.

Jaffar bellowed a loud laugh in disbelief.

"You must be kidding! Why in the world would I do that? Father and I must obtain the secret of the Golden Clock before them!"

Slanted sunbeams shined through the large glass windows onto the grand marble table. Uncle Idris stared at Jaffar in deep thought. He paced the dining hall back and forth with his arms crossed over his chest. Despite his short stature, he carried himself in a dignified manner and had a calming presence to him. He stroked his long, thin white beard. Jaffar had never seen his uncle so serious. It was always his father Khan that was the more serious brother.

It seemed like forever before Uncle Idris finally spoke again.

"For the first time, I am not joking, my son." He walked up close to Jaffar and placed his hand on his nephew's shoulder. They were almost at eye level. Uncle Idris continued, "Your father is the one who wants to obtain the secret of the Golden Clock, not you. You only want to please your father. In the process, you are becoming someone you are not. This is not how your mother raised you."

The mention of his mother made Jaffar furious. He could feel his face turning red as if his blood was boiling.

"My dear uncle, please do not mention her to me again!" Jaffar was panting with anger. He knew his mother was alive and had not passed away like he thought, thanks to the letter his sister Jasmin finally showed him after all these years. The thought of her just getting up and leaving her family deeply pained Jaffar.

"She still loves you so much and prays all night for you and Jasmin," said Uncle Idris adjusting the small white cap on his head.

Jaffar felt as if he had been hit by a ton of bricks.

"*What*? You are still in touch with her? How could you keep this from me? All these years I thought she was dead, only to find out that she just left us!"

He now had an awful feeling in his throat and could feel his eyes welling up with tears. However, Jaffar refused to shed any more tears for the mother that had abandoned him.

"You really think that's what happened?" Uncle Idris was more serious than Jaffar had ever seen him. His eyes bulged, the red veins more noticeable than before. Uncle Idris pulled out a chair from the dining table and placed his stout body onto it.

"Jaffar? Jaffar! Where are you? Are you in here?"

Just then, Jaffar's father Khan walked into the

14

dining hall. He froze at the sight of his elder brother sitting solemnly at the table.

"What are *you* doing here?!" shouted Khan. "You know you are not allowed to set foot into this house!"

A dark vein protruded out of Khan's forehead. Jaffar feared for his uncle who he loved dearly.

Uncle Idris looked up at Khan, without moving from his seat. His eyes were fearless and intense piercing back at his brother. His beard moved up and down as he slowly uttered to his brother, "I came to see my only nephew and forewarn him that the Jannah Jewels are coming here, *next.*"

3

The List

"Who's next?" Sensei Elle addressed her students. She stood before them with her bow and arrow in hand, with perfect posture, like a cement pillar holding up a house.

Hidayah stood up. Her face was glowing against the dawn's golden hues. "May I go next, Sensei?"

Sensei bowed her head and lowered her eyes affirmatively. Her red robes flowed gently in the morning breeze.

Hidayah positioned her bow and arrow on her back, placed her foot in the stirrup, and climbed on top of Iman's horse Spirit.

NEIGH!

Hidayah bent forward and lowered herself to his ears, which he kept moving to and fro. She stroked his mane as he snorted nervously.

"*Bismillah*, Spirit," Hidayah whispered softly into his ears. "You can do this. We've been training every day. Just follow my lead."

Spirit stomped his hoof multiple times.

Hidayah straightened her back, grabbed the reigns, squeezed the sides of Spirit with her knees and lightly tapped him with her foot. Spirit began to trot then quickly cantor and then rapidly gallop. Hidayah started riding towards the target placed high up in the maple tree. The wind smacked against her face and the ends of her *hijab* danced gracefully behind her. She released the reigns from her hands and grabbed the bow and arrow from her back. She let her knees steer Spirit.

Then Hidayah anchored her arrow into the bow and gently pulled back the string with her first two fingers. She took a deep breath and lowered the arrow until it was even with her heart. She felt as if she was flying as she cleared her mind and her heart.

I am one with the bow, thought Hidayah closing her eyes. *Ya Allah, help me to never miss my mark*, she silently prayed.

"*Bismillah!*" she shouted as she released the arrow and heard it slice through the wind.

A few seconds later, there was an outburst of cheers and applause.

"Go, Hidayah! *Masha Allah!*" shouted Iman, Jaide, and Sara along with the other dojo students.

Spirit came to a slow stop. Hidayah opened her eyes and looked up at the target high above her. There sat her arrow: right in the center. She smiled and whispered, "*Alhamdullilah.*"

As Hidayah rode back to her friends, she patted Spirit with contentment and pride. After the intensity of the last mission, Hidayah had worked diligently with Spirit to train hard for what may be next.

"That was unbelievable!" screamed Jaide as Hidayah pulled up to the stables. "I still can't get over how you ride and shoot at the same time!"

18

"*Masha Allah*, Hidayah. You made Sensei and the other Masters very proud today," told Iman. "They made *du'a* that Allah continues to increase you."

The Jannah Jewels all hummed '*Ameen*' together. Hidayah felt humbled and grateful to her Lord. She quickly and quietly made a *du'a* in her heart to always keep her intentions and actions purely for Allah's sake.

"They asked to see us right away at the time-traveling maple tree," said Sara.

"Let's go!" said Hidayah with a new burst of energy. She scooted forward to make room for Iman. Jaide and Sara hopped onto Jaide's skateboard. The Jannah Jewels rode quickly down the hill to the park where their favorite tree stood. To their surprise, all four Masters were waiting for them. They were quietly sitting together in a circle knee-to-knee at the foot of the tree.

As the girls approached the Masters, Sensei Elle looked up at them.

"You must take Spirit with you," she said as she arose.

The other Masters then stood up and aligned themselves with Sensei Elle.

"My dear Jannah Jewels, this will be your toughest journey yet," spoke the Master Swimmer. "It is unlike any journey you have taken thus far and will take great endurance. When you face darkness, know that Allah is *An-Nur* and will bring you into light." She locked eyes with Sara.

All four girls' eyes sparkled as they listened very attentively.

"You will have to face many challenges with this mission," warned the Master Artist. "Know that the world is your canvas. If Allah wills it, you can paint anything."

Jaide nodded.

"Use Allah as your Guide," reminded the Master Rider while looking at Iman. "When you are lost, turn to Him for direction." She rubbed the stripe on the bridge of Spirit's nose. He nickered contently.

"You will be travelling to Fes, Morocco," Sensei Elle informed the Jannah Jewels. "You must stick together and not let the beauty of the ancient, walled city deter you from your purpose. Keep your focus on the mission and avoid Jaffar and his family at all cost."

She paused here.

Why is she mentioning his family? wondered Hidayah. *We've only dealt with his sister Jasmin so far. Adults can't time travel anyway,* she remembered. *So who else is Sensei talking about?*

Sensei handed Sara a folded piece of paper and bunches of mint leaves. Sara looked at the writing on the paper. It was in French. It looked like a list of rules or guidelines that read:

1. Don't judge a fruit by its scent.

2. Find your senses.

3. Blood is thicker than water.

4. Dig deep.

5. Charity shields.

Sara wondered why the list was in French if they were heading to the African continent, but she would not dare question the Sensei. She placed the list into her pocket and the mint leaves into her backpack.

"These will help you on your mission to find the ancient artifact and return home safely," said Sensei Elle. "Now go. We are but a number of days. Time is either with us or against us. May Allah put *barakah* in your time."

Hidayah clucked her tongue signaling Spirit to move right up to the maple tree. Jaide and Sara grabbed on to each side of Spirit's head collar. Then all four Jannah Jewels closed their eyes and held on to Spirit tightly. In unison, they recited, *"Bismillah-ir-Rahman-ir-Raheem!"*

4

Sweet Smells

The Jannah Jewels stood atop a small hill covered with dried dirt and tiny scattered rocks. The soft morning sunlight gave the hill a bright orange tint. The air smelled dusty and warm but carried a gentle breeze that circulated the hill. Iman's horse Spirit was a few meters away grazing on little spurts of grass peeking out of the ground.

They were standing next to a wide tree with big thick thorny branches that stemmed from its short, gnarled trunk close to the ground. The branches looked as if they had been flattened from one side and the leaves looked leathery.

MAA! MAA!

The girls quickly turned around and looked up into the tree.

"Are those what I think they are?!" Jaide asked pointing at a colorful herd of goats. "I have got to make a sketch of this!" she said pulling out her sketchpad and artist pen from her backpack.

"*Subhan Allah!* screamed Iman. "Look at all those goats!" She started counting the number of goats standing on the tree's branches munching on its fruits and leaves. Iman let out a happy laugh. "There are nine goats hanging out in that tree! *As salaamu alaikum!*" she greeted the goats.

MAA! MAA!

"Aww. They just replied 'peace be upon you too,'" Iman shared with the girls.

"This must be '*Eid* for you, Iman," Jaide teased the animal-lover while putting her sketchbook and artist pen away. "Get it? Goats! *'Eid*! Ahahahaha!" She held her stomach as she laughed hard at her own joke.

Sara playfully slapped Jaide's shoulder. "Wow, you must really be hungry if you've got such awful

25

jokes this early in the morning," she said smirking at Jaide.

"Hey! We scrambled out of Vancouver without eating any breakfast! Of course I'm hungry!"

"I can't believe this tree can hold up all these goats!" Hidayah interrupted. She was amazed at the sight. Some of the goats had climbed all the way to the top of the tree. It looked surreal.

"This is an argan tree," said Iman while looking at her *Book of Knowledge*. "It has very deep roots that protect the soil and can draw water from 100 feet below. It can grow 8-10 meters high and can live anywhere from 150 to 200 years!"

All the girls stared up at the tree with even more amazement.

"I wonder what that fruit is that the goats are enjoying so much," said Jaide. "I want to try some!"

Before the Jannah Jewels could stop her, Jaide was already climbing up the trunk and balancing herself along a goat-free branch to grab one of the tree's small oval-shaped fruits. She yanked 4 fruits off the branch and carefully climbed back down.

"They look like little lemons!" Jaide said holding them out in her palms to her friends whose mouths were watering now.

Then immediately, Hidayah shook her head.

"I don't know if we should eat them though," Hidayah protested. "I don't feel right about this."

Iman and Sara nodded in agreement. The Jannah Jewels always trusted Hidayah's judgment greatly.

"Plus we don't know who this tree belongs to," added Sara, who was very in-sync with the environment. "We can't just take from someone else's provisions."

"I don't see the goats hesitating to eat from that tree," Jaide argued.

Her stomach was starting to growl with hunger now. Jaide looked around the hill to see if anyone was around. She saw a tall boy with a slight limp walking up towards them holding a staff in his right hand. He was lean and wore a dusty, long, beige hooded-robe with a turban wrapped like a ring around his curly-haired head. As he walked up closer to them, he dried the sweat off his face with the tail of his turban.

"I'll just ask that kid if he knows who the tree belongs to," Jaide said pointing to the dark-skinned fellow.

Hidayah, Iman, and Sara all gathered next to Jaide.

Then Iman whispered softly to the group, "Remember Sensei told us to stay focused on our mission. Let's not forget why we are here."

"*As salaamu alaikum! Ahlan wa sahlan*, my sisters!"

His words could not have been more welcoming. His pure-white smile contrasted his skin and dusty garb, and he was even taller up-close. He carried a strong scent of perfume and wore a string of *tasbih* beads around his wrist. His eyes were lined with kohl.

Hidayah looked down at his large feet and noticed he was barefoot. She wondered which era this could be and how old he was. She figured he must be around 9 or 10 years old.

"My name is Mus'ab. Can I help you with

anything?" the boy had switched from Arabic to French.

Jaide nudged her elbow into Sara's side and pushed her forward to the front of the girls.

"Answer him!" she ordered Sara.

Sara stood frozen. She was surprised to hear him speak French.

"Sara! Ask him if he knows whose tree this is, and if we can eat its fruits! I'm starving!" Jaide's anxious tone brought Sara back to her senses.

"Um…*wa alaikum as salaam,* brother," Sara spoke hesitantly as she was not used to speaking French outside her home. "My name is Sara, and these are my friends Hidayah, Iman and Jaide. We are new in town and were wondering if you know who owns this tree. We would like to eat some fruit from it. We are very hungry," she stated hoping he understood her 21st century dialect.

His face suddenly became dismal.

"I would not do that if I were you," he responded. "It may smell sweet, but it has a very unpleasant flavor."

29

The first rule! Sara reached into her pocket and pulled out the list of Sensei's guidelines to help the Jannah Jewels along this mission. She re-read the first line:

1. Don't judge a fruit by its scent.

Mus'ab spoke again, "If you are hungry, please come have breakfast with my family and me. We live right there at the bottom of the hill. My mother just asked me to come up and round up our goats from our tree. She will be so happy to see you all. She loves visitors."

He was smiling at them again, but Hidayah, Iman, and Jaide noticed Sara's expression become weary.

"What's he saying?" Iman asked Sara.

"He's warning us that the fruit smells good but tastes bad," she informed them. "He is inviting us to breakfast at his home instead."

Jaide's face lit up. "I'm in!" She was always ready for free food.

"Please excuse us for a second," Sara gestured

to Mus'ab politely and pulled the girls a few feet away from him.

The goats began to make noise in protest as Mus'ab used his staff to guide them down from the tree. His height definitely helped him reach even the highest-climbing goats.

"I don't know if we can trust this guy," Sara warned her friends in a soft voice.

"Why not?" asked Jaide. "He seems harmless and smells like sandalwood."

"Wait! Look at this, girls!" said Sara.

She showed them the paper with the mission's guidelines.

"Sensei's first rule warns us not to judge a fruit by its scent!" Sara translated to the other Jannah Jewels. "At first I thought she may have been referring to the argan tree fruit, but what if she meant in terms of trusting people?"

"Maybe Sara is right," Hidayah said in agreement. "We learned from our last mission not to jump to conclusions. Now we should maybe be careful who we can trust for help as well."

Hidayah's own words hit her hard. A strong feeling came over her heart.

Be careful who we can trust for help.

MAA! MAA!

The goats had surrounded the Jannah Jewels. They were gnawing at Jaide's hands that were still holding on to the little yellow-green fruits. Each of the girls grabbed a fruit and started feeding the goats. All four of them laughed as the goats' wet, warm tongues tickled their palms.

"This one's my favorite," Iman said pointing at an orange, long-haired goat. The goat rubbed her coat against Iman's leg. She bent down and patted the goat's side.

MAA!

"Oh mi gosh! Guys! She says we can trust Mus'ab!" Iman shouted over the blare of the goats. "She says he is a good master!"

The Jannah Jewels all smiled with relief.

Mus'ab limped over to them.

"Did you call me?" he asked in English.

They all stared at him.

"Wait, you speak English too?" Sara asked him.

"Yes, my mother has taught me Arabic, French and English, *Alhamdullilah*."

The girls were all impressed.

"Oh that's great! Well, we decided to accept your invitation *in sha Allah*. Thank you *Jazak Allah khair,* for inviting us."

"*Alhamdullilah*, that's wonderful! I'll just tell my mom you all are coming."

The Jannah Jewels all stared at Mus'ab with confusion.

"And how will you do that?" Sara questioned him.

Mus'ab laughed with a puzzled tone. "What century are you guys from?" he asked them jokingly. He reached into his robe's pocket and pulled out a cell phone.

"I'll just call her, of course!"

5

Game Changer

Jaffar did not know who to call on for help anymore. His beloved uncle, the only person Jaffar felt he could really trust in his life, had shocked him with two blows. The first being that he still had contact with Jaffar's mother, which meant his uncle probably knew her whereabouts. Second was that the Jannah Jewels were now coming to Jaffar's hometown of Fes.

He tried to make sense of it all.

How could the Jannah Jewels be coming to Fes? he thought. *Are they coming after Jasmin and me? Is the next artifact right here in Fes? Are they coming to present-day Fes or traveling back in time as usual? How did Uncle Idris know they are coming?*

He tried to wrap his head around all these questions he had and ignore the worrisome feeling stirring in his heart. *I am not scared of them*, Jaffar told himself. *This time, I won't let the Jannah Jewels get away. This is my turf! Enough is enough!*

Jaffar stared at the map spread out in front of him on the dining table. Indeed, the next artifact was marked above his own city.

How could I miss that? he wondered. He could not tell what the artifact was. It just looked like an oval-shaped dark blob. *Not again*, he thought. His sister Jasmin and he had had enough trouble in ancient Spain last time. They could not figure out what type of powder was in the vial for the ancient artifact. He only knew it was something red, yet came back empty-handed and badly defeated by the Jannah Jewels.

Part of Jaffar did not even really care much about the artifacts anymore. He had grown tired of all this chasing and fighting to discover the Golden

Clock's secret. He missed just being a kid, sitting under the mango tree in the courtyard, practicing his calligraphy and reading his favorite books.

A few moments later, Uncle Idris entered back into the dining hall.

"It's time, Jaffar." he told him. "Your father has prepared everything to face the Jannah Jewels. Those girls are no match for your father's anger and greed. You must help them."

Jaffar tried to make sense of his uncle's words. He temporarily forgot about being upset with him.

"Father is going to face them? Himself?" he asked.

"Yes, my son," answered Uncle Idris. "I should never have told your father they were coming. I don't know what came over me. I really try not to let my anger get the best of me; it's a family weakness and a constant struggle for me."

A strange rush of concern came over Jaffar. He remembered Hidayah saving him from drowning in the ocean back in China. He knew his uncle was right. The Jannah Jewels were no match for his father who was a great warrior and archer and knew how to use his skills against people to get his way.

"This is not his fight," spoke Jaffar. "We must stop him."

Jaffar grabbed Uncle Idris by the hand and pulled him out the door. They ran quickly together down the long corridor decorated with priceless paintings and old weapons that were family heirlooms passed down for generations, which Khan greatly treasured. Neither Jaffar nor Uncle Idris ever really cared much for them. They hardly even noticed them as they whizzed past them.

They rushed out into the great courtyard. It was nicely shaded and filled with beautiful gardens, luscious fruit trees, strings of lanterns and a large stone circular fountain in the center. This used to be Jaffar's favorite place in the house as he had helped his mother build it from scratch and would play with her and Jasmin for hours here as a kid. It had been a long time since he had visited this courtyard.

Khan was standing near the mango tree with his students huddled around him all carrying bows and arrows on their backs.

"There are four of them, and they will be travelling together," he informed them. "If any of you see a group of these foreign little girls, bring them to me," he instructed. "They have something that belongs to me, and I must get it from them." He handed each of them a small square packet. "If you get a hold of any of them, use this." The students read some writing on the packets and then nodded affirmatively in unison.

"Father, what are you doing?!" Jaffar shouted.

Uncle Idris was still holding his hand and squeezed it tightly. Jaffar turned and looked at him. His uncle had a look of plea in his eyes as if he was silently saying, '*Choose your words wisely.*'

Jaffar took a moment to recollect himself. He remembered his mother's advice to send prayers upon the Prophet, peace and blessings be upon him, whenever he was too angry or upset.

"*Allahumma sali 'ala Sayidina Muhammad,*" he whispered softly. Uncle Idris heard Jaffar's whisper and smiled gently with content. With his uncle by his side, Jaffar walked up slowly to his father.

"Father, why are you doing this?" he questioned Khan, who looked down at his son in disregard. "Let me deal with the Jannah Jewels. I know how to fight them, and I will not let them get away this time."

Khan seemed unusually composed. He calmly yet in a firm manner replied, "I have given you enough chances. You have greatly let me down. Now it's time for me to take matters into my own hands."

"Khan, they are just little girls," Uncle Idris broke in. "What if someone was going after your own daughter, God forbid? They are someone's daughters too. You have *already* lost so much. You mustn't give up your dignity too."

There was a thick silence amongst all the men. Khan's face formed an unpleasant grimace. He knew what his older brother was implying.

"Let's go," he said as he signaled his small army of men to head out of the courtyard. They followed him like a band of lemurs.

"Father! Please stop!" Jaffar screamed, but

Khan did not even look back at his son or elder brother. He continued to march forward and exited the courtyard through the narrow brick doorway onto the outer streets.

"We have to do something! We need to find the Jannah Jewels before he does!" Jaffar ordered Uncle Idris in a panic.

"Now that sounds more like the nephew I know and love!" proclaimed Uncle Idris placing both his pudgy hands on Jaffar's two shoulders. "I knew you'd come around!" He pulled Jaffar close and wrapped his short arms tightly around him.

Jaffar returned his warm hug for a quick moment. "Let's not lose our focus here, Uncle Idris!" he said escaping out of his uncle's strong grip. "What are we going to do?"

"Okay, let's think for a second," Uncle Idris responded. "You, Jasmin, Moe and Slim are the only ones that know how the four Jannah Jewels look, so that gives us an advantage. Now we must get those three to help us without giving away too much."

"And how will we do that?"

"Leave that up to me," Uncle Idris said with a confident smile. "Where there's Allah, there's a way!"

6

The Maze

"There is no way!" said Jaide in disbelief. She could not believe how they had only traveled through space, not time.

The Jannah Jewels watched how easily Mus'ab gathered up his goats from the argan tree and guided them down the hill, even with his limp. The Jannah Jewels followed the boy and watched in awe how he gently used his staff to steer and nudge the goats toward his home.

"Girls, what's the plan?" Iman softly asked as she pulled Spirit behind her. They were all walking slowly together behind Mus'ab.

"We're going to get some Moroccan grub!" Jaide

chimed in.

"Okay, but then what? We can't be here all day! We are on a mission, remember? We need to figure out what the next artifact is and where to find it," insisted Iman.

"Sara, can you tell Mus'ab we will be down in a few minutes?" asked Hidayah. "Tell him we just need to gather our things."

Sara nodded and did just that. Mus'ab pointed at which house was his and then waved at the Jannah Jewels.

Sara walked back to the others. "He says that's fine but not to be long," she told them.

The four friends quickly sat down in a circle, and Spirit began to graze again next to them. Iman pulled out her *Book of Knowledge* from her bag while Hidayah took out the ancient map from its bamboo case. She spread it out onto the hard ground in the middle of their circle.

Pointing to the sixth artifact, Hidayah spoke, "So, it's not very clear what we are looking for *again*. It just looks like a dark-colored oval object." They

43

all sighed in frustration. "What does the *Book of Knowledge* tell us about the city of Fes, Iman?"

Iman was already sifting through the pages. She stopped on a section displaying a beautiful green and white ancient building. She placed the book on top of the map. "Well, Fes happens to be the home of the world's oldest existing university! This is the University of al-Qarawiyine built and founded in 859 by a woman named Fatima al-Fihri," said Iman showing the girls its picture in the book.

"The ancient artifact is probably in there somewhere!" guessed Sara.

"Yeah, that seems like a great place to start," added Jaide hastily. "Now can we hurry up and go eat already?"

"Okay, maybe Mus'ab or his mom can help us get there," Hidayah said.

"Let me also translate the rest of Sensei's list for you guys," said Sara as she pulled out the paper from her pocket. "That way we are all on the same page and can keep an eye out for any of these clues."

She read the list out loud:

1. Don't judge a fruit by its scent.

2. Find your senses.

3. Blood is thicker than water.

4. Dig deep.

5. Charity shields.

"What does all that even mean?" asked Jaide. She was jotting the list quickly into her sketchpad.

Sara shrugged her shoulders.

"That's what we have to find out," Hidayah said with determination. "Let's go."

The Jannah Jewels put their things away and started walking alongside Spirit. They walked slowly down the hill together taking in the beautiful sights of the city in front of them. The homes were all close together aligned on short hills throughout the city and numerous minarets stood out lining the sky. The city was enclosed inside an old stone wall just as Sensei Elle had described it.

As they approached Mus'ab's home, he signaled them to enter the open field behind his house where the goats were grazing along with some chickens and roosters. It was a very simple, old-looking home from the outside. A tall, lean woman stood at the back door waving a fan in front of her sun-kissed face. A bracelet made of seeds dangled from her wrist. She wore a bright *hijab* on her head and a long cotton *abaya*. She smiled brightly as she squinted her eyes from the morning sunlight.

Something about this woman reminds me of Sensei Elle, thought Hidayah.

"You can leave your horse here to rest," Mu'sab told the girls. "I'll bring him some water," he said as he limped toward his house. His mother quickly walked over to the Jannah Jewels.

"*As salaamu alaikum! Ahlan wa sahlan!*" she greeted them happily. She walked up to each girl, grabbing her by the sides of her face and placing a warm kiss on each of her cheeks.

"*Walaikum as salaam!*" they each responded with big smiles.

"Please come in!" she welcomed them.

The Jewels entered through the back door as Mus'ab was walking out with a pale of water for

Spirit. The girls were astonished as they walked into a breath-taking, beautiful square courtyard. Hidayah, Iman, Jaide and Sara looked around in wonderment.

"*Subhan Allah*! This is amazing," Sara said.

Hidayah had to do a double take. The courtyard seemed to come out of nowhere based on the look of the house from the outside. It had a sudden calmness to it. It was in the center of the home surrounded by tall pointy archways leading to different sections of the house. It was full of green plants and trees, a bunch of little fountains and bird baths, colorful tile flooring and dark, narrow wooden framed doors with horizontal sliding metals locks. Above it was a wooden balcony that wrapped all the way around the courtyard. To the corner, shaded under part of the balcony, was a long rectangular wooden table low to the ground with thick cushions lining the floor all around it. The table was adorned with an array of breads, drinks, fruits, eggs, cheeses, oils, butters, soups, spices, pastries, vegetables, and yogurts.

This must be what Jannah looks like, thought Hidayah.

Jaide started making her way to the table with her mouth wide open. Hidayah grabbed her by her backpack and pulled her back.

"Forgive me for not having a proper meal ready for you," Mus'ab's mother spoke.

Iman spoke first and said, "We are so grateful to you and your family for welcoming us into your lovely home on such short notice. We did not mean to trouble you in any way."

"Not at all. It's our pleasure. What are your names by the way, and where are you all from?" the kind, iridescent woman asked gesturing the girls to take their seats around the table.

Hidayah, Jaide and Sara felt really warm all of a sudden with nervousness. They all looked at Iman with concern as they slowly made their way around the breakfast table.

"My name is Iman, and these are my close friends Hidayah, Jaide and Sara." There was an obvious hesitation in her voice. "We are from Canada. We really want to visit al-Qarawiyine."

"That's a beautiful mosque," Mus'ab had joined

them in the courtyard now. "One of Fes' original treasures," he said proudly as he poured each of the girls some mint tea.

"Would you be able to take us there after breakfast?" Sara asked him.

"Sure, *in sha Allah*," he responded. "I have to take lunch for my brothers who study at the university there. You can all join me."

"Oh, how many brothers do you have?" asked Hidayah.

"Two. Amin and Sadiq. They are twins."

Mus'ab's mother's eyes lit up at the mention of her elder sons' names. She told the girls how the boys had to memorize the entire *Holy Qur'an*, as well as a book of narrations of the Prophet Muhammad, peace and blessings be upon him, an Islamic law book and an Arabic book all by the age of 15 before they could gain acceptance into the university.

"Mus'ab will be following in his brothers' footsteps too," she told them. "He is almost done memorizing the *Holy Book*, *Alhamdullilah*."

"Where does he study?" asked Iman.

His mother smiled humbly. "At home with me," she answered with a shy smile.

"*Masha Allah*! You've memorized the whole *Qur'an*?

All four Jannah Jewels' eyes were on Mus'ab's mother. She lowered her gaze and nodded.

"She taught my brothers as well," Mus'ab added. "She helped them memorize all the prerequisite books."

"Wow! *Masha Allah*, you are such an inspiration!" Jaide said with her mouth full of fresh-baked pita.

The boy's mother simply thanked Allah for all His blessings and kindness. In the short period of time together during breakfast, the Jannah Jewels not only ate well, but also learned that their hosts were of Berber descent coming from a lineage of farmers, traders, and nomads, that Mus'ab's mother was a widow who supported her family from the sales of argan oil from their argan tree, and Mus'ab had gotten his limp after falling out of the tree when he was little.

"He is always looking for adventure, this one," his mother told them.

If he only knew of the adventures we go on, thought Hidayah laughing to herself.

The Jannah Jewels helped clean up after breakfast. Iman continued to have one-on-one conversations with Mus'ab's mother finding out more about her work, how she extracts argan oil from the tree's fruit and how she finds time to balance being a mother and teacher to her boys alongside working. All the while they packed lunches for her twins.

Mus'ab led the girls out towards the front of the house, grabbed the lunch sacks and kissed his mother good-bye on her hand.

Each of the girls thanked their host and took *du'as* from her.

"We can't thank you enough," said Hidayah. "This has been such an honor for us. You welcomed us with such love and inspired us greatly in such a short amount of time, yet we don't even know your name."

"Please. Call me Umm Amin," she answered.

"And just remember my family and me in your *du'as*, especially while you travel as the traveler's *du'a* is always accepted."

The Jannah Jewels nodded and smiled bidding farewell. Hidayah and Iman climbed onto Spirit while Jaide and Sara walked alongside following Mus'ab onto the unpaved street.

No one said much as they headed towards the medina. It had been such a beautiful morning thus far, and the girls continued to enjoy its blessings. They each silently did *dhikr* and recited, *"La ilaha ill Allah."*

"So, the part of the city that we are in is called Fes el Bali," Mus'ab finally spoke up turning back to look at the girls. "It is known to be the biggest car-free urban zone in the world! The most modern thing we have here is probably electricity."

They approached the ancient and mysterious great stone wall that enclosed the medina and its large arched gateway leading to numerous shops and many tiny, narrow walkways that looked like a giant maze. Behind the wall, sticking out from the center of the maze stood a tall green and white minaret.

"Which mosque is that?" Iman asked Mus'ab pointing to the minaret.

"That's al-Qarawiyine, where we are headed," he answered. "You have to go down, down, down to the center of the medina to reach it."

"Can we take Spirit inside?" she questioned him.

"Yes, mules and horses can fit through the walkways. It's still early so the bazaar is not so busy. Once we get to al-Qarawiyine, I can have one of my brothers watch your horse or we can tie him up to a pole or something," he said. "There are some 9,000 streets and alleyways here, so stick together. It's easy to get lost."

As they made their way slowly through the great stoned arch gate, the Jannah Jewels became mesmerized for time seemed to be suspended here.

The city looks so old and medieval, Hidayah thought. She felt as if they really had traveled back in time.

The streets were mostly calm except for some mules carrying in goods to the shops on their backs. There were ancient fountains lining the walls all over the streets.

"Are these for making *wudhu*?" asked Sara.

"Yes," said Mus'ab. "They were created by engineers in the 11th and 12th centuries and are still used efficiently to this day."

"Let's all refresh our *wudhu*," suggested Sara. "I want to see how these work."

"Great idea," said Jaide. "These look so cool!"

Iman dismounted Spirit but not Hidayah, who had a look of worry across her face. She wanted to keep an eye out for Jaffar and his gang in case they showed up.

"I made *wudhu* before we left Mus'ab's house," she told them as she scanned the maze cautiously.

Mus'ab showed Iman, Jaide, and Sara how to turn the fountain on, and the three of them joyfully performed ablution with the cold, fresh water. Hidayah watched them with content looking around every so often. She then noticed a short, stout bearded man with a small white cap on his large bald head standing outside a perfume shop a good distance away staring at her with his eyes squinted.

Is he looking at us? Hidayah wondered and turned around to see if anyone else happened to be behind her. No one was behind them. When she looked back at the old man, there stood Jaffar next to him whispering something into his ear. Hidayah's heart sank to her stomach. The other Jannah Jewels had their backs faced towards Jaffar and had no idea what was going on as they wiped their faces and arms with water.

The old man walked back, and then Hidayah saw Jasmin, Moe, and Slim further behind Jaffar searching the maze. The short man went up to them looking frantic and escorted them in the opposite direction away from the Jannah Jewels.

Who was that? Where is he taking them? she thought.

By this time, Jaffar was running towards them full speed. He did not seem angry, though, like usual. This time, there was a look of worry on his face. Nevertheless, Hidayah knew where there's Jaffar, there's trouble.

"You guys! It's Jaffar! Run!" Hidayah screamed.

The girls were suddenly alarmed as they were in midst of washing their feet in the fountain. They each lost their balance and fell back onto the ground.

Mus'ab dropped the lunch sacks and quickly helped Iman get up first.

"Hurry! Get on!" Hidayah ordered. She grabbed Iman's hand as she lifted her skirt and climbed on top of Spirit as fast as she could. Spirit became startled and lifted himself onto his hind legs neighing loudly. Hidayah and Iman held on tightly to his back as he started racing back out of the maze.

"What's going on? Who's Jaffar?" Mus'ab asked in a panic now helping Jaide and Sara onto their feet.

"There's no time to explain!" Jaide answered grabbing her skateboard from her back. "We need to go! Now!" Jaide pulled Sara and Mus'ab onto her skateboard and took off steering through the maze.

"Oh no! What about Hidayah and Iman?" Sara asked worriedly looking back.

"Jannah Jewels! Stop!" Jaffar called out to them. By the time he reached the *wudhu* fountain, all four Jannah Jewels had escaped. He bent forward putting his hands on his thighs trying to catch his breath.

Spirit was deathly spooked and rode on hastily up the hill. Iman turned back to look at Jaffar standing panting in the distance near the entrance of the maze. Sara, Jaide, and Mus'ab were nowhere in sight.

"Iman! How do I get him to stop?" Hidayah shouted.

Iman looked forward again and grabbed hold of the reigns from Hidayah and yanked them back.

"Spirit! Stop in the name of Allah!" she commanded him. Spirit slowed down to a calm trot then stopped fully.

NEIGH!

"*Alhamdullilah!*" Hidayah sighed gratefully. She stroked his mane, and Iman patted his side as they both slipped down off Spirit's back.

"That was so close! And we lost the others! Where could they have gone? Sensei told us to stick together, and we didn't!" Iman cried out looking winded and almost in tears. "What are we going to do now?"

"Don't worry, Iman. Allah will help us get through this. We will find them *in sha Allah*," Hidayah reassured her. "You guys didn't see but Jasmin, Moe and Slim were there too along with some old man, who was the one who originally spotted us. He whisked them away before they could see us. I don't understand why that man did that. Then, only Jaffar came towards us, and strangely enough, he didn't seem to look upset today but more worried."

Iman was not processing any of Hidayah's words. She was still in shock. There was intense worry and fear spread across her face as she scoped their surroundings for any more surprises.

Hidayah grabbed hold of both of Iman's shoulders and locked eyes with her hard.

"Iman, listen to me," she shook her. "We---will---

find---them. They have Mus'ab with them who knows his way around."

Tears were streaming down Iman's face now and blurring her vision through her glasses. Hidayah was scared too but stayed strong knowing they had Allah with them at all times. She reminded Iman of what the Master Rider had advised them.

"Remember what the Master Rider said?" she asked her. "She said that when you are lost, turn to Allah as your Guide. *Al-Hadi* will guide us through this. Don't worry. Come on now. Let's go back to Umm Amin," Hidayah ordered. "I'm sure she can help us find our way through the maze and figure out how to find the others *in sha Allah*.

A sense of relief came over Iman. She sniffed and wiped the tears from her cheeks and cleaned her glasses with her shirt. She gave Hidayah a timid smile of agreement.

"Why don't you get on Spirit first since you are so good with him?" Hidayah suggested. She helped Iman pick herself up and get back on top of the horse. She remembered part of a saying of the Prophet, peace and blessings be upon him, where he said to give charity even by helping a person climb her mount.

Please God, accept this deed as a charity and let it be a shield of protection for us, she prayed in her heart thinking of one of the guidelines on Sensei's list.

After Iman was safely seated atop Spirit, Hidayah heard a familiar sharp '*whoosh*' whiz past her ear. She looked down to see that an arrow had just missed her.

Not wasting a second, she jumped onto Spirit holding on tightly to Iman and screamed, "Go! Go! Go!"

Spirit took off again galloping swiftly through the rough fields of tiny pebbles and dry grass.

"What's wrong?" Iman shouted through the muffling wind, startled again.

Hidayah pulled out her bow and arrow ready to fire back and carefully turned around expecting to see Jaffar again. To her surprise, it was not him at all.

Instead, there she stood glaring at them as angry as ever in her gray flowing robes with her bow in her hands. It was Jasmin.

7

Overwhelming Odors

"Sisters! Please! Someone tell me what's going on!" Mus'ab loudly pleaded gripping Sara's shoulders for dear life. Jaide, Sara, and Mus'ab zipped through the dizzying alleyways in the bazaar. The end of Sara's *hijab* waved crazily through the air and slapped Mus'ab in the face. He whipped back grabbing hold of his turban with one hand to prevent it from flying off his head.

Jaide did not know where they were headed, but she followed her heart and zoomed her skateboard this way and that to get them as far away from Jaffar as fast as possible.

"There was someone coming after us," Sara told

Mus'ab as they dashed past all the different *souks*. As if the danger they were trying to escape was not enough, Sara was starting to feel queasy from the rainbow of sights and smells rushing at them.

There were endless shops with stalls set up outside in the narrow walkways. The shops were shaded underneath short canopies throughout the maze. They sped and skid through the shoe district, the sweet *souk*, past the meat stalls, perfume shops, the spice market, tables full of sunglasses, dates, oils, combs, leather handbags, and rimless hats. They saw quick glimpses of master artisans meticulously working with specialized tools and their bare hands creating beautiful rugs, pottery, furniture, slippers, baskets, and other fantastic goods.

Jaide dodged chickens, pigeons, cats, shoppers, merchants, and tourists as she rapidly got hit with whiffs of raw meat, essential oils, cumin seeds, barbeque smoke, fresh fish, and yeast. Oddly enough, it was all making her hungry again, but she kept her focus on maneuvering her board sharply through the streets.

Know that the world is your canvas. If God wills it, you can paint anything, she remembered the empowering words of the Master Artist. As she weaved in and out of the maze's late-morning crowd, Jaide imagined her skateboard to be a giant artist pen that she was using to scribble on the earth with her wheels. The speed and thrill of the ride was invigorating.

"Where are you going? Al-Qarawiyine is not this way!" Mus'ab shouted waving his arms up and down to get Jaide's attention from the back of the skateboard.

Just as Jaide was about to turn around to make sense of Mus'ab's words, the skateboard abruptly came to a sudden stop. The three of them were catapulted through the air.

"Ahhhhh! Hold on!" screamed Jaide.

They frantically waved their limbs trying to grab hold of each other as they soared higher and higher upwards.

"Please God! Lighten our fall!" shrieked Sara.

As fast as they had gone up, they came down

even faster.

"Look out!" Mus'ab shouted.

BOOM! CRASH! BANG!

The three of them had collided into a make-shift structure of wooden scaffolding. Large pieces of wooden boards, poles, and canopies tumbled down. Dust and debris flew everywhere.

Jaide, Sara, and Mus'ab lay scattered under all the rubble. Their heads were spinning, and their bodies ached. Each moaned in pain.

There were screams and shouts of concern nearby. A small group of shopkeepers came rushing to the scene. They slowly moved pieces of wreckage off each of them.

"Are you all okay?" an elderly man asked Jaide.

She hazily stared up at his face trying to register what he was saying and what had just happened. He carefully helped her sit up. She could taste dirt and gritty sand in her mouth as she coughed profusely and gasped for some clean air.

"My friends..." she spoke coarsely looking for

Sara and Mus'ab worriedly through the cloud of dust and shards around her. Then she heard Sara cough and moan close by her. Mus'ab's scratchy voice was also not too far from her. As she looked around, she could not believe she had done this to them. Her head hurt, and her heart ached. Jaide shielded her eyes as the African sun was blinding at its zenith point.

The onlookers slowly helped each of them to their feet. Jaide, Sara, and Mus'ab painstakingly limped over to each other. They were unrecognizable. The three of them were covered in dust with small cuts and wounds. The girls helped wipe each other off and with soreness adjusted their *hijabs*. Mus'ab used the cloth from his unraveled turban to clean his face and neck.

"You guys are walking like me now," Mus'ab teased.

The girls both let out short reluctant giggles.

"I'm so sorry," Jaide apologized holding back her tears. "I don't know how this happened. I was controlling my skateboard just fine."

A small crowd of worried onlookers was still standing around them. Sara noticed a short, little boy at the front of the crowd holding Jaide's board. She sluggishly walked over to him and kindly asked to have the board back. As she examined the board, she was shocked at what she found.

"Jaide! Mus'ab! Look at this!" she exclaimed.

Sara flipped the skateboard upside down revealing the bottom of the board. There, jammed in the front right wheel was a sharp, thin arrow.

Mus'ab glared at the girls fearfully.

"Why is there trouble following you girls?" he asked looking at them like they were complete strangers. "Who are you girls, and what is all this?" he asked wide-eyed with bewilderment.

Sara looked at Jaide who gave her an '*it's okay*' nod.

"We are the Jannah Jewels," Sara informed him in a soft voice. "We travel through time and space on missions in search of ancient artifacts to solve the secret of a Golden Clock and save the world from getting into the wrong hands."

Mus'ab's dusty face became white, and his jaw dropped. Jaide and Sara gave each other a quick glance wondering if they had told him too much. By now, the crowd around them had begun to disperse.

Before Mus'ab could respond, he noticed through the crowd a familiar-looking tall, lean man with a salt-and-pepper colored beard staring hard at them with dark, piercing eyes. He had a bow in his hand and a group of men following him as he rapidly made his way pushing through the crowd towards them. Mus'ab realized that was Fes' leading archer Khan and knew everyone in town stayed clear of him. Mus'ab grabbed the board out of Sara's hands, broke the arrow in half, and yanked it out of the sides of the wheel.

"Uh oh! Looks like trouble again! Jaide! Drive!"

He pushed the board into Jaide's arms. Forgetting all about her pain, Jaide tossed the board down to the ground pulling Sara and Mus'ab onto it with her again. She sped up to a fallen wooden plank that had anchored itself perfectly as a ramp and used it to help them fly over the rubble leaving a trail of grainy dust behind them.

Sara turned back to see what the 'trouble' was. She saw a bunch of men running after them.

"Get them!" the elder leader ordered.

The young men lined up in a row and one-by-one started shooting arrows at them.

"Jaide! You gotta get us outta here!" Sara screamed. "Some men are firing arrows at us!"

Jaide swerved the skateboard side to side as fast as she could to dart the shower of arrows coming at them. She saw a narrow, dark alley to her left and quickly steered the board to it.

As they rode through the alley, the stench in the air was overwhelming. The three of them quickly covered their noses and mouths with their palms. The further in they skated, the more intense the pungent odors became. Nearing the end of the alley, Jaide pressed one foot hard against the ground and let it drag bringing the skateboard to a stop. Mus'ab and Sara stepped off the board finding their balance as they placed their feet back on solid ground.

The alleyway had led them into an open arena with a giant honeycomb of deep, circular stone vessel pits in it. There were men immersed waist-deep in the colored pits diligently working with large pieces of fabric. It reminded Jaide of an enormous human-sized pallet of water colors.

The smell did not seem to bother the men at all. However, Jaide and Sara quickly covered their noses with the ends of their *hijabs*, while Mus'ab used his turban cloth.

"Where are we?" Jaide muffled her words through her scarf as she looked out into the honeycomb.

"Whaaaatttt did you say?" Sara muffled back.

Jaide turned towards Sara and lifted her scarf away from her mouth still keeping her nose covered. "I said *where are we*?!" she shouted.

"This is the ancient Chouara leather tannery," Mus'ab answered through his cloth. He turned back to make sure they were not being followed anymore.

"I wish we had something to block off this smell," suggested Jaide. "I think I'm going to be sick." She could feel Umm Amin's lavish breakfast coming back

70

up.

Sara then remembered the mint bouquets Sensei had given before they left Vancouver. She reached into her backpack and pulled out three of the aromatic mint bouquets and handed them out.

"Quick! Stuff these into your noses!" she ordered.

They each grabbed hold of a bunch and pressed it up into their nostrils. Jaide, Sara, and Mus'ab briefly laughed at how silly they looked. The smell of fresh mint brought about a feeling of homesickness for the girls as they sniffed the leaves and remembered sipping Hidayah's famous mint tea back at the dojo.

"I hope Hidayah and Iman are okay," said Sara nasally, her smile vanishing.

"I'm sure they are fine *in sha Allah*," Jaide replied. "I'm more worried about who those men were that were chasing after us!"

"That was Khan, a great archer of Fes," Mus'ab informed them. "No one messes with him. How did you end up getting on his bad side?"

The girls shrugged their shoulders.

The three of them looked around the huge honeycomb to make sure the coast was clear. There were spectators looking down from old, wooden terraces hovering all around the tannery and some men laying out dyed fabrics to dry on the open rooftops. Thankfully, nobody looked dangerous.

"How do we get out of here?" Sara asked with urgency.

"I'm not sure," Mus'ab answered. "Let's ask one of the workers."

"I feel so bad for them," said Jaide. "They are out in this open heat, without any machinery, literally swimming in dyes."

"They love what they do," Mus'ab corrected her. "The leather is cured almost the same as 1,000 years ago and made into goods. The tannery is run by one family, and the dying technique has been passed down from generation to generation."

Sara's eyes lit up.

"The list!" she exclaimed. She quickly pulled Sensei's list out of her pocket. "There's a reason we ended up here. I know it," she said showing the list to Jaide and Mus'ab.

Mus'ab read the list but looked dumbfounded.

"I don't get it," he said confusingly.

"Our Sensei gave us this list to guide us on our mission. Look!" Sara pointed to rules 3 and 4. "*Blood is thicker than water*. That must have to do with the tannery's family. And *dig deep*…"

"…Must have to do with the tannery's deep vessels of dye!" Jaide concluded for her. The girls gave each other high fives full of glee.

"I still don't get it," Mus'ab said scratching his frizzy-haired head.

"The artifact just might be here!" Sara tried explaining.

"Ooo. *Don't judge a fruit by its scent!*" added Jaide.

"Okay, now you're just pushing it," Sara spoke.

"Hey, you never know! All these clues are so mysterious," Jaide shrugged her shoulders. She grabbed Sara by the hand and led her to one of the workers kneading animal hides with his bare feet inside one of the red dye pits. "Come on! Let's hurry and figure out why we are here before trouble finds us again!" she hastened and signaled Mus'ab to follow them.

Jaide pushed Sara forward to initiate a conversation with the dark, sweat-ridden man. He had a thick, brown mustache that spilled over his upper lip.

"*As salaamu alaikum*," Sara spoke nervously. "We are looking for a small brown-colored oval object. Do you know if we can find something like that here?"

"*Walaikum as salaam*," the tired man replied with a sincere smile. "My wife may be able to help you. She helps collect material for the dyes," he said pointing to a small, cracked wooden door.

"*Jazak Allah khair*," said Sara.

They quickly walked back to the door, which was ajar. They knocked and waited outside. A few moments later, a short, energetic woman came to the door with mint leaves stuffed in her nostrils as well. Despite the fatigue on her face, she welcomed

them with a warm smile.

"*Masha Allah!* Such beautiful children! May God's Peace be upon you. What can I do for you?" she asked cheerfully.

Sara repeated her question and told the woman that her husband had sent them. The woman nodded and led them to the back of her quarters to a concrete-walled room full of stored raw materials.

"I don't have all our materials here right now," she said. "There is not enough space to keep them all here. I do have some seeds, flowers, powders, and oils with me, though," the woman said laying a few things out onto a wooden bench.

Jaide, Sara, and Mus'ab examined the materials carefully.

"What's that?" asked Jaide, pointing towards a dark-colored polygon-shaped seed.

"That's the seed for a henna plant," she told them. "We use henna to make orange dyes, a 6,000-year-old practice. Once its seed is planted deep, its blossoms grow with such a beautiful fragrance. Did you know that was the favorite scent of the Prophet, peace and blessings be upon him?" the woman shared proudly.

They each shook their heads. Jaide and Sara looked at each other with contentment as they both thought of Sensei's guideline again of *dig deep*.

"How can we get one of these seeds?" Sara asked.

The woman took a small handful and placed it into Sara's palm.

"Take these my dear. Please accept them as a gift from our family," the woman said.

Sara was smiling again.

"Your family is doing great things," she said placing the seeds in her pocket. "May God continue to put *barakah* in your work," prayed Sara.

"*Ameen*," the woman replied joyfully lifting her eyes and hands to the air.

The three of them thanked her again, asked how to exit the tannery and politely excused themselves out. Jaide and Sara felt overjoyed that they had found the ancient artifact.

As they walked out of Chouara, they found themselves outside a lonesome perfume shop. They each let out a sigh of relief as the friendly shopkeeper rubbed perfume on the back of their hands.

Mus'ab brought his hand to his nose to sniff the perfume only to realize that the mint was still stuffed up his nostrils.

"I think we can take these out now," Mus'ab said pointing at his nose and laughing.

The girls nodded as they watched the shopkeeper head back inside. Just as they removed the leaves from their noses, the three were unexpectedly grabbed from behind. Jaide, Sara, and Mus'ab tried to scream but could not let out any sound. White square cloths were being pressed against their faces. Then, suddenly, everything became completely black.

8

Trapped

Khan's black eyes stared hard at Jaffar.

"What exactly did you think you were doing?" Khan asked interrogating him. "They all separated from each other."

Jaffar glanced at his sister standing in the corner and then looked back down at his sweaty hands.

"I was trying to stop them," he mumbled.

Khan's long black robe moved about his ankles as he paced his bedroom back and forth.

"You are not telling me the truth," he said firmly to his son. "Jasmin told me that you and Idris were up to something. What was it?"

"Tell the truth, Jaffar!" the words spit out of Jasmin's mouth. "You had Uncle Idris divert Moe, Slim and me away so you can get the artifact from the Jannah Jewels first! I should have known you never wanted my help," she said darting anger at her brother with her gray eyes.

Jaffar could feel his face getting hot. He sat on the edge of his father's bed knocking his knees together. He locked eyes with Khan's for a second, only to quickly look down again. He remained silent.

"Answer me!" demanded Khan.

The bed shook as Jaffar trembled. He wished his uncle was with him at this moment, but Khan had his guards escort Uncle Idris off the premises.

"It doesn't matter," Jaffar nervously spoke. "They got away."

"That's what you think," Khan said with a half-smirk. "I should have known if I want something done right, I must do it myself."

Extreme worry came over Jaffar. He looked up at his father fretfully.

"What do you mean?" Jaffar was standing now.

Khan looked over at Jasmin and gestured her to leave.

"I'll meet you down there," he told her.

Jasmin gave one last mean look to Jaffar and stormed out of the room, her gray robes flowing behind her.

Khan stroked his black-and-white beard. His face was expressionless.

"It's my good fortune that I had to go nowhere, and the great Jannah Jewels came right to me," he said curtly. "No more wild goose chases. I'm going to put an end to this game myself."

"What are you going to do to the Jannah Jewels?!" Jaffar was stiff with anger.

"That's none of your concern. Go back to your calligraphy and artwork. Jasmin and I will take it from here." Khan briskly walked out locking the door behind him.

Jaffar ran to stop his father, but it was too late. He was trapped.

****

Sara felt trapped. She awoke to a fainted ringing sound. The ground beneath her was cold and hard. The air was thick and smelled of mold and sweat. It was completely dark. She could not see a thing. The ringing became louder and louder.

"A phone!" she came to her senses and realized where the sound was coming from. "Mus'ab! Are you in here? Answer your phone!"

"Huh? Huh? Where are we?"

SMACK!

"Ow!" Mus'ab rubbed his head. He was too tall to sit up properly in the tiny space. "I should have brought my helmet if I knew what type of trouble you guys would get me into."

His phone stopped ringing.

"Jaide! Jaide! Are you in here? Wake up!" Sara carefully sat up and felt around the tight area looking for her best friend. She found Jaide's leg nearby and shook it.

Jaide opened her eyes.

"Ahh! I can't see!"

"Shhh. Calm down. Someone will hear us!" Sara loudly whispered.

"Where are we? What happened? Why is it so dark?" Jaide rubbed her eyes trying to see in the dark.

"I think we were kidnapped," Sara speculated. "This feels like some type of cellar or something."

Jaide gasped. "Kidnapped?!" She began to cry. "I don't know how much more of this I can take. I'm hungry. I'm thirsty. I'm tired. I'm in pain. I miss Hidayah and Iman. I miss eating my mom's chicken dumplings. I miss home," she sniffed back her tears.

"Mus'ab, can you call your mom or brothers for help?" Sara asked while comforting Jaide and handing her the water canteen from her waist belt. "Here. Drink up," she instructed Jaide.

Mus'ab felt for his phone in his robe's pocket and checked the call log.

"She just called!" he said with relief.

He quickly dialed her back.

"Salaam Ummi! Ummi, we need help! We've been kidnapped! We don't know where we are! We're trapped in some really dark place!"

Sara and Jaide listened to traces of Umm Amin's worried voice on the other end of the call. Mus'ab was alert and listened to his mother carefully.

"Hello? Hello? Ummi?!"

Mus'ab shut his phone in frustration. "Urgh! My phone died."

Jaide began to cry again.

"Don't worry girls," said Mus'ab. "My mother said Hidayah and Iman are with her, and they will find us. She told us to call onto *An-Nur* to help us while we wait."

When you face darkness, know that Allah is An-Nur and will bring you into light.

Sara suddenly remembered the guiding words of her beloved Master Swimmer.

"Let's do *dhikr* of Allah then," she suggested.

Each of them silently called on God's name of Light repeating '*Ya Nur, Ya Nur*' to themselves.

Mus'ab used the *tasbih* beads wrapped around his wrist to keep count.

After a few minutes, Sara's back began to hurt sitting stiffly on the hard uneven floor. She slipped off her backpack and slammed it against the stone ground. All of a sudden, a light shined brightly through the fabric of her bag.

"What is that?" Jaide asked excitedly.

Sara slowly opened her backpack and pulled out the light. "My metal ball! It's a flashlight!"

"*Subhan Allah!* Look at that!" Jaide exclaimed.

Sara moved the ball of light around the space. They were sitting in a small crevice with a low concrete ceiling and short walls.

"How do we get out of here?" asked Mus'ab. "And how did we ever fit in here?"

"There!" Sara pointed the light towards a small wooden door above their heads. "Push!"

The three of them tried to push the tiny door with all their might.

"Urgh! It's no use! It's locked!" said Mus'ab.

"Wait! I know!" Jaide grabbed her artist pen out of her backpack. "Maybe I can pick the lock with this." She fiddled the tip of her pen in the tiny keyhole as Sara shined the light from her metal ball onto it. "Please open it, *Ya Fatah*," Jaide whispered.

CLICK!

"Alhamdullilah! It worked!" Sara screeched. "How'd you think of that?"

Jaide finally smiled big. "I remembered how Hidayah picked that lock in the dark tunnel back in Spain with her arrow tip. Being in the pitch dark must have also awakened my senses, because, I thought of Sensei's guideline to 'find your senses,' so I used my sense of judgment and my sixth sense you could say." She squinted playfully.

Sara gave her a look of impressiveness. "Well then, let's thank God for our sense of sight and common sense," she noted.

They all softly whispered, *"Alhamdullilah."*

The girls sighed with relief. Sara tapped her metal ball firmly to turn off its flashlight and placed it back in her backpack. Then, with Mus'ab behind them, they all quickly crawled out of the small space and found themselves in a large, empty kitchen inside someone's home. They squinted as their eyes adjusted from darkness to the bright midday sunlight pouring in through the kitchen's tall glass windows. The aroma of warm soup and fresh-baked bread filled their lungs.

"Mmm. It's lunchtime," whispered Jaide licking her lips.

"Focus!" Sara scolded her.

Scoping the area, they saw a door leading out of the house towards the back of the kitchen.

"That way," Jaide pointed.

They tip-toed across the kitchen floor to the distant exit. Their hearts raced with fear.

"Father! They're escaping!" a familiar voice screamed from behind.

They slowly turned around to find an angry Jasmin standing behind them.

"There are guards all around the house. You aren't going anywhere."

Fast, hard footsteps came stomping towards the kitchen. Khan blasted through the door.

"Where are they?!" Khan was panting with fury. He turned to find three sets of petrified eyes staring at him. Immediately, his expression changed to an eerie grin. "Well, well, well. If it isn't the famous Jannah Jewels…well, half of you anyway!" he said gliding over to them. "It's a pleasure to finally meet you. Welcome to Fes." His words carried a tone of mischief in them.

Jaide, Sara, and Mus'ab breathed heavily as they looked up at their kidnapper's face.

"You've met my son and daughter already. I'm Khan, their father. We briefly met earlier in the maze if you recall," he let out a deep laugh. "It's a shame you're not all together. Where could the other two have gone?"

"Even if we know, we would never tell you," Mus'ab spoke up boldly. Jaide and Sara looked over at him with astonishment.

"And who are you exactly?" Khan asked towering over Mus'ab.

"I'm a helper."

Khan let out a loud cynical laugh. "A helper, eh? So then you must know where the artifact is, oh great young helper."

Mus'ab kept his gaze on Khan without cowering. He did not say another word.

"Tell me, boy!" shouted Khan shaking Mus'ab harshly.

"Stop!" pleaded Sara. "He doesn't have it! I do!"

Khan released Mus'ab's shoulders and stared hard at Sara. "Jasmin, check her!" he ordered his daughter.

Before Jasmin could walk over to her, Sara reached into her pocket and took out the henna plant seeds.

"That won't be necessary," she said. "These are it," Sara said holding out the seeds in her open palm.

"You expect me to believe *those* are the ancient artifact? Do I look like a fool?" he struck Sara's hand sending the seeds flying all over the tiled floor. Sara cringed in fear.

"That's enough, Father!"

An awkward silence thickened the air. Khan looked as if he was ready to explode with anger. He peered over the Jannah Jewels' heads, and there stood Jaffar behind them. He was standing at the door leading from the outside of the house into the kitchen.

"Jaffar? How did *you* get down here?" Khan pushed Sara aside, knocking her to the floor, and wrathfully walked up to his son.

Jaide quickly bent down to assist Sara back onto her feet. As she lowered herself, Sara reached up grabbing Jaide's skateboard from its carrier on her back. She placed it on the kitchen floor and forcefully pushed it toward Khan as he walked towards Jaffar.

"Father, look out!" Jasmin shouted.

"Huh?" Khan turned around abruptly only to suddenly fall backwards. The speeding skateboard knocked him off his feet, flying him up then pounding him hard onto his back, his head whacking against the marble tile. He was immediately knocked out.

"Father!" cried Jaffar as he crouched down to

shake him awake.

"Now's our chance!" screamed Sara. She pulled Jaide and Mus'ab by the hands toward the exit.

"Oh no, you don't!" Jasmin launched towards them to stop them from escaping, not seeing the open cellar door on her way. She fell feet first right into the small opening in the floor.

"Ahhh!" she screamed landing with a loud thud onto the concrete cellar floor below.

Sara, Jaide and Mus'ab leaped over Jaffar and Khan, Jaide grabbed her skateboard along the way, and they raced straight out the door. As they ran out, arrows came flying at them from all corners. Jaide shoved Sara and Mus'ab behind her pressing them against the side of the house and used her board as a shield.

"*Ya Arhamar Rahimeen*, please help us, Allah!" she screamed as arrows bounced off her board one after the other.

Suddenly, there were loud yells coming from all around. The arrows stopped attacking the three of them. In that moment, they looked up to see

what was happening. Charging through the desert perched high on Spirit rode Iman, Umm Amin and Hidayah. Khan's men were falling to the ground one by one as Hidayah bravely fired arrows into their shoes. An echo of grown men crying in pain filled the air. Jaide, Sara, and Mus'ab hopped onto the skateboard and sped to Hidayah and them as fast as they could, cheering and shouting along the way. The horse riders dismounted and ran over. Umm Amin pulled Mus'ab into her arms. Hidayah and Iman immediately stopped to look at Jaide and Sara with shock. They were covered in dust and scrapes, and their *hijabs* were torn all over.

"Are you guys okay?" Hidayah asked with deep concern on her face. "What happened to you two?"

"*Alhamdullilah*, we are safe! We can't thank God enough," Sara responded still a little shaken from their close escape. "And we are so happy to see you guys again! How did you manage to find us?"

"Thank God that Umm Amin was able to track Mus'ab's phone," Iman told them.

The girls all embraced one another and shared

quick exchanges of gratefulness and endearment. By the will of God, the Jannah Jewels were reunited once again.

9

Herstory

The reunion was short-lived. As hugs, kisses, tears and laughter flew all around, Jaide caught her eyes on her wrist. She had totally forgotten to check her time-traveling watch.

"You guys. We only have an hour left to get back home!" she announced forgetting that Mus'ab and Umm Amin were there.

"An hour? To Canada?" asked Umm Amin puzzled.

The Jannah Jewels all looked at each other nervously.

She has helped us so much. She deserves to know the truth, thought Hidayah.

"Ummi, these are not just any girls," Mus'ab spoke up. "They are the Jannah Jewels on a mission to restore peace on Earth."

Umm Amin absorbed her son's words surprisingly well. "I knew you all were special the moment I saw you. Light radiates from each of your faces *masha Allah*," she said.

"As does yours," replied Hidayah genuinely. She then turned to Jaide and Sara. "Iman and I were not able to find anything that resembled the ancient artifact. How about you guys?"

Sara's eyes welled up with tears. Jaide laid her hand on Sara's shoulder to console her.

"We had found henna plant seeds in this giant tannery, but Jaffar's father Khan didn't believe them to be the ancient artifact and hit them out of Sara's hand," Jaide relayed the story. "I don't think we have time to go searching for them again," she said.

"How do you know for sure those were it, though?" Iman asked. "Remember what we learned from our last mission in Cordoba not to jump to conclusions. As odd as it may seem, maybe Khan

96

was right."

Hidayah remembered their original plan. "We have not checked al-Qarawiyine yet like we had first planned," she reminded them. "Umm Amin, how fast can we get there from here?" Hidayah asked her.

"On horseback and the skateboard, maybe fifteen minutes or so, *in sha Allah*," Umm Amin speculated.

"Ummi, don't get mad, though," Mus'ab's voice hesitated. "But I dropped Amin and Sadiq's lunch sacks somewhere in the bazaar."

They all burst out in a relief of laughter.

"Let's not worry about that right now," Umm Amin responded with a smile. "First, let's help these Jannah Jewels save the world!" she said with new determination.

Led by Umm Amin steering Spirit's reigns, the new team rode and skated as fast as possible to al-Qarawiyine. The maze was much more crowded this time of day. They swayed carefully through the crowd as they went down, down, down to the center of the maze. Jaide weaved through the bazaar like an expert now.

They approached a wide set of tiled stairs leading up to a majestic green and white ancient building.

"I was scared you'd break my good leg!" Mus'ab said jokingly as he stepped off Jaide's board. "This is the fastest I have ever reached al-Qarawiyine! I have got to get me one of these!"

Jaide smiled at him proudly as she tucked her skateboard under one arm.

"We're here!" Iman screeched and leaped off Spirit. She clasped her hands together jumping up and down excitedly.

Jaide had already pulled out her sketchpad and artist pen and was busy sketching her view of the beautiful mosque from the bottom of the staircase.

Hidayah and Umm Amin then dismounted Spirit.

"Umm Amin, we are looking for an ancient artifact that might be here," Hidayah told her. "We are not sure what it is, but it's shaped like an oval and has a dark brown color."

Umm Amin had a look of deep thought.

"I'm not sure what it could be," she replied. "Where do you want to look first: the mosque, the university, or the library?"

The girls' eyes lit up.

"How about all three?" Iman suggested smiling ear-to-ear.

"But we only have 45 minutes left!" added Jaide displaying her watch to everyone.

The call for *Dhuhr* prayer came from atop the great mosque then echoed through the bazaar.

They all stood quietly to listen to the chorus of the call to prayer, the *'athaan,* being called from the many different minarets throughout the medina. When the call was done, they each silently made intense *du'a* as they knew this was a time of accepted prayers.

Please God, please let Jaffar's father be okay, Sara quietly prayed for Khan despite the trouble he had put them through.

"Now that we have heard the call to prayer, we need to answer it. We can't leave without praying *Dhuhr*," Hidayah noted. "We will pray and then

99

quickly search around for the artifact."

The group nodded in agreement. Sara helped Iman tie Spirit to a lamp post nearby.

Mus'ab decided to go find his brothers. "I'll meet you guys back here after *Dhuhr*," he said as he left.

Umm Amin and the Jannah Jewels slipped off their shoes, grabbed them with their left hands and entered through the heavy gates of the grand structure with their right feet.

"Welcome to al-Qarawiyine!" Umm Amin addressed them.

The Jannah Jewels were awe-stricken. They walked into an open courtyard full of diamond-patterned tile flooring. It felt cool to the touch, a pleasant change from the desert heat.

There were clean, white tall horseshoe archways surrounding the entire courtyard. Dark green terracotta roofing adorned its top. Beautiful lanterns, carved wooden trimmings, and perfect geometric patterns outlined the walls. A flower-shaped fountain stood in the courtyard where men were making *wudhu*. There were melodious voices of people reciting *Qur'an* together throughout the facility.

"Al-Qarawiyine was built by a Tunisian immigrant named Fatima al-Fihri in 859 AD," Umm Amin informed them as they all toured around. "She used all her inheritance to fund its building and directly overlooked the construction process, paying attention to every intricate architectural detail. She was a woman of deep faith who fasted everyday for two years until the construction was complete. Building this university helped transform Fes into a major intellectual, cultural, and spiritual center for the Muslim world and the West. In only a few decades, the University of al-Qarawiyine became a leading institution of learning that attracted great thinkers, scientists, philosophers, physicians, mathematicians, writers and historians from all around the world like Pope Sylvester II, Maimonides, Averroes, Ibn Khaldun, and Leo Africanus, to name a few."

"*Subhan Allah!* How amazing it would have been if we met her," said Iman. "She changed *her*story forever."

"She really did," added Hidayah as she looked around. "This place is simply beautiful, *masha Allah*. So much detail everywhere, and it's so big! It reminds me so much of Spain."

The Jannah Jewels felt as if time was frozen here.

The congregation began to assemble in the prayer hall, and everyone placed their shoes in wooden cubbies against the back wall. The girls quickly made *wudhu* and joined Umm Amin with other female worshippers lined up on straw mats. As the *imam* began the prayer, the Jannah Jewels raised their hands and pushed all their worries behind them. They each soaked in the serenity of the silent prayer. Jaide and Sara felt a sense of relief after the intense encounter with Khan and his men.

After the prayer ended, Iman noticed a scrawny, stray cat sitting next to her. She smiled and greeted the cat with peace, petting her gently. The cat purred with delight making Iman giggle. Jaide and Sara crowded around to see what Iman was doing. They all started playing with the cat, chasing her around the prayer hall. They quickly became so immersed that they completely forgot about keeping track of the time.

Meanwhile, Umm Amin and Hidayah remained sitting quietly side-by-side still enjoying the feeling of worship and doing silent *dhikr*. Hidayah felt a familiar connection to Umm Amin as she sat close to her, like she had always known her. She turned slightly to take a quick glance at her up-close and noticed how her features and skin tone were very similar to Sensei Elle's.

Then the cat calmly walked over to Umm Amin who began to pet it.

MEOW!

"Aww, she really likes you," Iman told Umm Amin as she followed the cat over to her.

The cat meowed again. Iman gasped.

"What's wrong?" asked Hidayah looking at Iman.

"She says Umm Amin has what we are looking for!" Iman shared with excitement.

"Me?" said Umm Amin with surprise.

"Yes!" answered Iman.

Umm Amin padded herself to see if she was carrying anything. "I don't have anything on me except this simple bracelet," she said lifting her wrist up in the air to show it and startling the cat away mistakenly.

Hidayah examined it carefully. It had a cluster of large brown oval-shaped nut kernels linked together by a thick clear wire.

"What are these?" she asked.

"These are kernels from the inside of argan fruits," she told them casually. "My boys made this for me when their father passed away."

"How sweet," said Jaide. "Is there something inside them?"

"Not in these; they are dried and empty," said Umm Amin slipping the bracelet off her hand. The kernels clattered against each other. "They usually have what we call 'liquid gold' inside their seeds."

"Liquid gold?" Sara asked. "What's that?"

Umm Amin gave a faint smile. "Argan oil. We

Berbers have been using it as medicine for centuries, but recently it has been tested to help reduce aging. The oil is worth a lot of money, so we call it liquid gold. The argan tree itself is an ancient species that has been around for millions of years. It lives for a long time because of its deep roots that search for water and anchor the tree saving it from wind damage. My family's tree has been there for almost a hundred years planted by my great-grandparents themselves!"

"Woah!" said Jaide. "Now *that's* ancient!"

They all shared a good laugh. Umm Amin handed the bracelet to Hidayah. "Go now and take this. You have brought so much joy to me today. I feel like Allah blessed me with four daughters. I know each of you will do great things. Allah chooses His workers wisely. I pray this bracelet will be a charity on behalf of my husband, my sons, my ancestors, and me *in sha Allah*."

Sara went through Sensei's list in her head. It was all coming together now.

Hidayah slid the bracelet over her hand and

onto her wrist. She did not want this moment to end.

Jaide checked her watch: only 17 minutes left to get home. She silently showed the others. The Jannah Jewels' hearts felt heavy. No one wanted to leave this place or leave Umm Amin. They each had tears streaming down their faces.

Umm Amin stood up, and the girls followed. She kissed each of them on the head.

"I must stay here and find some lunch for my two older boys," she smiled. "I'm sure Mus'ab is waiting outside for you," she told them. "He will guide you back out of the maze."

"Will we ever get to see you again?" Hidayah sniffed through her words.

"If not in this life, then surely I'll meet my blessed Jewels again in Jannah," she reassured them. "Now go. May Allah continue to be with you."

The four of them quickly hugged Umm Amin, grabbed their shoes, and ran out looking for Mus'ab. He was waiting with Spirit right where he said he would.

"Mus'ab, you must help us get back to your argan tree right now!" Hidayah spoke in a panic. "Please!"

"Okay, but only if I get to drive the skateboard," he replied with a sly smirk.

"What? No way!" Jaide disputed.

All eyes were on Jaide. Everyone knew no one was allowed to touch her skateboard, but they looked at her with desperation.

"Uff! Fine! You are acting just like how my little brother does! We have no time to waste right now! Only 11 minutes left, people!" Jaide announced in frustration.

She reluctantly handed her board over to Mus'ab and jumped on behind him with Sara. Hidayah and Iman quickly untied and mounted Spirit. The five of them soared through the bazaar in no time. Mus'ab led them out of the maze smoothly, and they all raced through the dry fields, past his house and up the hill to the same argan tree. It was decorated with goats once again. As they walked up to the tree, the orange long-haired goat trotted over to Iman.

MAA!

"*As salaamu alaikum.* I missed you too," she said while petting and hugging the goat.

"Her name is Shams, because she reminds me of the sun," Mus'ab said smiling.

"Only two minutes left," Jaide spoke frantically. "We couldn't have done it without you, Mus'ab, and that sure was some awesome skate-boarding!"

"Yes, you truly were a great helper for us," added Sara.

"How can we ever thank you?" Hidayah asked panting.

"I know how," said Jaide. She handed him her skateboard.

Aside from everyone trying to catch their breaths, there was sudden silence. All eyes were on Jaide again: shocked.

"I can't take this," Mus'ab refused.

"God knows if we'll ever meet again," responded Jaide. "It will always remind you of what an adventure we had today. I'd be honored if you kept it," she insisted.

Mus'ab was beaming with joy as he held the skateboard studying it carefully.

"Woah, it still has marks from the arrows you saved us from…cool!"

The Jannah Jewels all laughed.

"*Jazak Allah khair*," he said humbly.

"*Jazak Allah khair* for all your help," replied Jaide.

"May Allah be with you all. Peace." Mus'ab gave a farewell wave, hopped onto his new skateboard and blissfully rolled down the hill back to his house.

Jaide looked at her watch. "Ten seconds."

The Jannah Jewels took one last look back at the beautiful ancient walled city, truly a city full of wonder, and gave their *salaam*. Together they pushed the trunk of the argan tree and down, down, down they went sliding through the tunnel.

When they reached the bottom, they joined hands and recited in harmony, *"Bismillah-ir-Rahman-ir-Raheem!"*

There was a great whirring sound. Then they

opened their eyes to a cool, familiar place. They were welcomed by the smell of maple in the air. The lanterns were dimly lit and quietness surrounded them.

Then, out of nowhere, the Jannah Jewels heard a loud noise.

MAA!

10

Keepsake

The girls spun around to see where the noise came from. To their surprise, Shams was standing behind them chewing on an argan fruit.

"Oh my gosh!" shrieked Iman. "She followed us home!" She hugged the goat tightly.

"What should we do with her?" asked Sara.

"Keep her!" Iman insisted.

"I don't know what Sensei Elle and the other Masters will say about this," Hidayah said with concern.

"Will say about what?" a soft voice spoke through the shadows. Sensei Elle walked up to the Jannah Jewels. Her face glowed even in the dim light. For a

second, Hidayah thought of Umm Amin again.

"*As salaamu alaikum*," they all greeted her.

"*Wa alaikum as salaam*," she replied.

"I don't know how this happened, Sensei," said Hidayah. "There were goats all over the Moroccan argan tree. I guess she followed us down the tunnel without us knowing."

"Everything happens for a reason," said Sensei Elle. Her eyes then fell on Jaide and Sara with sudden concern. "Before we discuss the goat, I want to know what happened to you two. I see you were greatly tested on this mission," she said to them. "Are you okay?"

"Yes, *Alhamdullilah*," they replied.

"God was with us all along the way, and He sent us a helper as well," said Jaide. "His name was Mus'ab."

"Sensei, I think Jaffar tried to help us too," added Sara. Hidayah and Iman became surprised at hearing this.

Be careful who we can trust for help, Hidayah

114

remembered her own words when they first arrived in Fes.

"Are you sure?" Hidayah asked Sara.

"Yes, he stood up to his father for us," Sara answered.

Sensei Elle smiled. Hidayah noticed a look of contentment on Sensei's face.

"Allah is the Changer of hearts," Sensei responded. "I had told you to find your senses. Your sense of judgment may be right, *in sha Allah*. Allah tells us in His *Holy Book*, 'Have you not seen how Allah presents an example: a good word is like a good tree, having its root firm and its branches [high] in the sky?'"

She then turned to Hidayah. "Were you able to find the sixth artifact?" asked Sensei Elle.

"Yes," said Hidayah removing Umm Amin's bracelet from her wrist. "We think this is it."

"You only need one of those kernels," Sensei told Hidayah. "Remove one and place it in the Golden Clock."

Hidayah untied the bracelet's string and carefully separated one kernel off of it. She then retied it and slipped it back onto her wrist. She walked up to the Clock and placed the oval-shaped kernel gently inside the empty space at the hour of six o'clock. The walls of the inside of the tree glowed from the bright light of the Golden Clock. It was a perfect fit.

"Congratulations, Jannah Jewels. You are officially half way there," said Sensei Elle.

The girls all hugged with excitement.

"May Allah accept all your hard work," Sensei prayed.

"*Ameen*," they hummed simultaneously.

MAA!

"What should we do with her? Can we keep her please?" asked Iman.

Sensei smiled and nodded in agreement.

"Yay! *Alhamdullilah!*" the girls cheered squeezing Shams with delight.

"Go rest for now. I'll take her and Spirit back to the dojo with me. You will need all your strength for your next mission. Peace be with you." And with those words Sensei Elle gracefully walked out of the tunnel, Shams trailing behind her.

"Can you believe it?" asked Iman. "She's our own little keepsake from Morocco! Allah is Al-*Kareem*!"

Sara, Jaide, and Hidayah all nodded with joy. Hidayah quietly fiddled with her bracelet. She realized she had been given a little keepsake of her own: a piece of another home, a piece of a family. She felt at peace.

"I wonder where we have to go next," said Sara.

"Please, let's not worry about that right now," pleaded Jaide. "I just want to go home. I miss my mom's dumplings and oddly my little brother too."

The girls all laughed as they walked out into the afternoon sun.

"Anyone else hungry?" asked Jaide.

"Me!" screamed Hidayah, Iman, and Sara.

"Too bad we don't have your skateboard to get us to your place faster," teased Sara.

"Who needs a skateboard, when we got these,

Alhamdullilah!" said Jaide pointing to her legs. "Race ya!"

And the Jannah Jewels giggled and ran together as fast as they could all the way down the street they all called home.

Don't miss the next Jannah Jewels book!

Will the girls have to face Khan and his men again? Does Jaffar truly want to help the Jannah Jewels or will Jasmin get to them first? Can Hidayah and her friends find the 7th ancient artifact in time to place it in the Golden Clock?

Find out in the next exciting adventure of the Jannah Jewels:

"Triumph in Turkey."

Find out more about the seventh book by visiting our website at <u>www.JannahJewels.com</u>

Glossary

Abaya: a long robe women wear

Ahlan wa sahlan: this Arabic expression comes from an old saying that shows Arab hospitality to strangers; 'ahlan means "family," as in "You've come to stay with family," and sahlan here means a flat land or plain where grass/food is abundant and to be shared with visitors.

Al-Hadi: a name of God in Arabic meaning 'The Guide'

Alhamdullilah: All praise is for Allah

Al-Kareem: a name of God in Arabic that means 'The Most Generous'

Ameen: Arabic word to close a supplication

An-Nur: a name of God in Arabic that means 'The Light'

As salaamu alaikum: Arabic greeting meaning 'Peace be upon you'

Barakah: blessing

Bismillah: Arabic for 'With the name of Allah'

Dhikr: remembrance of Allah

Dhuhr: the second prayer of the day

Du'a: supplication

'Eid: an Islamic holiday

Fajr: the first obligatory prayer of the day at dawn

Hijab: head-covering

Imam: the person that leads a congregation in prayer

Have you not seen how Allah presents an example: a good word is like a good tree, having its root firm and its branches [high] in the sky? (Surah Ibrahim 14:24)

Insha Allah: If Allah wills it

Jazak Allah khair: May Allah reward you with goodness

La ilaha ill Allah: Arabic for 'there is no God but God'

Masha Allah: Arabic for 'Allah has willed it thus.'

Quran: The last holy scripture of the Muslims.

Souks: Arabic word for 'markets'

Tahajjud: the frame of time within the last third of the night

And of the night, prostrate yourself to Him and glorify Him during the long night. (Surah al-Insaan 76:26)

Tasbih beads: beads tied together by a string to help keep count of one's supplications

Wa laikum as salaam: Arabic for 'and Peace be upon you'

Wudhu: ablution

Ya Arharmar Rahimeen: Arabic for 'O The Most Merciful of the Merciful'

Ya Fatah: Arabic for addressing God by His name 'The Opener'

122

JAIDE

To find out more about our other books,

go to:

www.JannahJewels.com